Stock Car
Drivers &
Tracks

Stock Car Drivers & Tracks

Featuring NASCAR's Greatest Drivers!

by Ken Spooner

PREMIUM PRESS AMERICA
NASHVILLE, TENNESSEE

Introduction

I was twelve years old when I met my first stock car driver heroes. It was in the pits of the legendary Islip Speedway, Long Island, NY. Already a BIG fan for two years, I saw up close for the first time two of the greatest drivers that ever ran there, Axel Anderson and Jimmy Hendrickson. NASCAR drivers were still 30 years away from the fame, fortune and celebrity that they enjoy today, but to this kid it was the same as if I had met Mickey Mantle or Willie Mays. I came away with an unforgettable experience that Sunday, the third of May, 1959.

Four years later I met another driver in the pits that would be another big inspiration for my brief racing career. He was bending over checking his lug nuts before going out to race against the likes of Fireball Roberts, Junior Johnson, Joe Weatherly, and Ned Jarrett. We struck up a brief but friendly one-on-one conversation and then I took my seat and watched him beat 30 some-odd Grand National Cars to the checkered flag on the Bridgehampton Road Course. His influence was so strong that I wound up painting his number on the door of my '37 Plymouth coupe. I was hoping it would help, as many other hopeful hotshots have done in the years since the prince turned into the King of Stock Car Racing. Once again I had a lifelong memory that just grows fonder as the years go by.

A little autograph book like this one sure would have come in handy back then. I hope it does for you and that you're able to fill it with 42 lifelong memories.

Dedication

This one's for a true champion, "Gentleman Jim" Hendrickson. He'll always be Jimmy to me and one of the best to ever turn a wheel anywhere. It's also for Marty "Nobody Has More Stuff" Himes. The best friend any racer could have anywhere.

Acknowledgements

George and Bette Schnitzer, NASCAR, Erik and Anne Spooner, Bill Caswell, and Uncle Axel.

Contents

DRIVERS

TRACKS

Loy Allen

Career Highlights

- First rookie to ever win the pole at Daytona, 1994

- 11th Place at the Coca Cola 600, 1994

Loy Allen

Loy Allen made history when he became the first rookie to capture the pole of the Daytona 500. Things have calmed down some since then, but a lot has to be chalked up to lack of experience. Loy hooked up with Junior Johnson in 1995.

Loy's big break came at Atlanta in 1992 when he won an ARCA race. The Hooters people were very impressed with the young charger and they backed him in the #27 car of Jr. Johnson's. He also is the highest finishing rookie in Daytona's history at 22nd. It shouldn't be long before pole positions become final positions for Loy.

Hometown: Raleigh, NC • **Birthday:** 4/7/66
Family: Single • **Car:** #27 Ford
Fan Club: P.O. Box 37011, Raleigh, NC 27627

John Andretti

Career Highlights

- First driver to ever compete in both Indy 500 and Coca Cola 600 on the same day, May 29, 1994!

- Won over $1 million in his first 64 career starts in NASCAR

John Andretti

When your father is Aldo, and your uncle is Mario, your cousin is Michael, and your godfather is A.J. Foyt, what else can you be when you grow up but a race car driver? John has competed in all types of cars. He started with the old modified coupes, then went on to midgets, sprints, Indy cars, dragsters, etc.

He really enjoys stock cars and all the people that race with and against him. His recent teaming with race veterans Kranefuss, Hass, and Brewer should be producing some up-front finishes very soon. But then with a name like Andretti, what else can John do?

Hometown: Indianapolis, IN ● **Birthday:** 3/12/63
Family: Nancy, Jarrett, Olivia Elizabeth ● **Car:** #37 K-Mart/Little Caesar's Ford
Fan Club: 2416 Music Valley Dr., Suite 161, Nashville, TN 37214

Brett Bodine

Career Highlights

- Won Union 400, 1990

- 2nd Place in Inaugural Brickyard 400, 1994

Brett Bodine

Brett is the second of the Bodine brothers to drive for Junior Johnson. He replaces the seat vacated by Bill Elliott. Brett has been able to run up front a lot and hopes the added reliability of Johnson's team and equipment will help carry him to some victories soon. Prior to the '96 season, Brett purchased the entire Jr. Johnson operation.

He began racing in 1977 at his family's track in upstate New York. He then joined the Busch series in 1985 and moved up to Winston in '86. His debut at the Coca-Cola 600 earned him the rookie of the race award. It appears that the personal problems that went public between him and Geoff on the racetrack have been resolved. Good luck to you, Brett Bodine, and to your new team.

Hometown: Chemung, NY • **Birthday:** 1/11/59
Family: Diane, Heidi • **Car:** #11 Lowe's Ford
Fan Club: N/A

Geoff Bodine

Career Highlights

- Won Daytona 500, 1986

- Won over $9 million in career

- Donated 1994 Busch Bonus to charity of Ernie Irvan's choice

Geoff Bodine

Modifieds . . . those 650 hp, short track Roman chariots of the 20th century, have produced some of the fastest drivers in NASCAR history. Geoff Bodine came to Winston from the Modifieds. I have heard some first-person accounts from the modified drivers who ran with Geoff in New York in the 60's & 70's. "What the heck does he got in there!" was just one of the phrases I've heard about Geoff's early days.

In 1993 Geoff purchased the race team of the late Alan Kulwicki and it has proven to be a smart move. He won $1.276 million in his first season with it. He also produces bobsleds for the USA Olympic team. They won a gold medal with it the first time out. You could hear the Russians saying, "What the heck do the Americans got in there? They got a BO-DYN, Boris, a BO-DYN!"

Hometown: Chemung, NY • **Birthday:** 4/18/49
Children: Matthew, Barry • **Car:** #7 Exide Ford
Fan Club: P.O. Box 1790, Monroe, NC 28111

Todd Bodine

Career Highlights

- Won the Winston Select Open, 1995

- Ran up front at Daytona till multi-car crash last two years

Todd Bodine

The youngest of the Bodine brothers got his start the same as the others, in the Modifieds of the Northeast. He found his way into a Winston ride by working on race teams. Moving to North Carolina, Todd started as a fabricator at Hendrick Motor Sports in 1986. When Butch Mock offered him a ride in '92, Todd took it.

He said he's learning every time out. When he was running up front in the '94 Daytona 500, Todd learned what happens when a bunch of guys get together at 180+ mph. In spite of some bad racing luck, Todd has had two top-5 and seven top-10 finishes in two years. His 69 Winston starts have netted him $1,225,666 in earnings. Keep an eye on Todd Bodine.

Hometown: Chemung, NY • **Birthday:** 2/27/64
Family: Lynn • **Car:** #75 Factory Stores of America Ford
Fan Club: N/A

Jeff Burton

Career Highlights

- Maxx Cards Rookie of the Year, 1994

- Won $1.2 million in 60 career starts

- Three Top-5's in three seasons

Jeff Burton

Jeff has gotten off to a good start in Winston Cup racing. Teaming up with the Stavola Brothers, he's qualified for every race except one where his car was disqualified for a rules violation. In both Pocono and Atlanta, he qualified 4th, and led at Atlanta for over half the race.

One of his biggest moments so far has been a 3rd place starting spot in the Winston Select and he held on pretty good, finishing up 4th in an all-star run for the checker. His biggest purse to date has been the $41,600 he collected at the first Brickyard 400. With career earnings from just 60 races at $1,235,020, I'd say Jeff has a bright future in Winston Cup.

Hometown: South Boston, VA • **Birthday:** 6/29/67
Family: Kim • **Car:** #8 Raybestos Ford
Fan Club: P.O. Box 339, Harrisburg, NC 28075

Ward Burton

Career Highlights

- Won first Winston Cup race at Rockingham, 1995

- Won the pole at the Mellow Yellow 500 in Charlotte, 1994

- Won $1 million in his first three years

Ward Burton

Engine problems. Nobody wants 'em, nobody needs 'em. Especially a rookie who's trying to prove himself to his fans, crew, and sponsor. And Ward has had his share his first year. In spite of this, he has done well when his car kept running. He has been very successful in the Busch series, where he won 3rd and finished in the standings. Perhaps when they get his engine sorted out, he'll do as well in Winston.

New crew chief Phillippe Lopez seems to be making a difference. Ward qualified for the outside pole and just barely lost to veteran Geoff Bodine in the All Star race at Pocono. His first year's earnings were over $300,000. They should increase as the problems get ironed out. Another guy to watch.

Hometown: South Boston, VA • **Birthday:** 10/25/61
Family: Tabitha, Sarah, Jeb • **Car:** #22 MBNA Pontiac
Fan Club: N/A

Derrike Cope

Career Highlights

- Won Daytona 500, 1990

- Won over $3 million in career

Derrike Cope

Derrike nearly gave the Bobby Allison team its first victory as an owner at Phoenix in 1995, but his tires gave out and he had to settle for second. But things are coming together for the Allison team, which has had much more than its share of hard times. Perhaps '96 will see them return to the winners' circle.

Derrike qualified the car for every race in the '95 season and finished 15th in the point standings. He also gave up his title of most eligible bachelor when he married a former Miss Winston, Renee White. A former pro baseball prospect, Derrike spends a lot of his time doing charity work both on and off season.

Hometown: Spanaway, WA • **Birthday:** 11/3/58
Family: Renee • **Car:** Team #12 Straight Arrow Ford
Fan Club: P.O. Box 1542, Cornelius, NC 28031

Wally Dallenbach

Career Highlights

- Career earnings over $1 million

- Best finish 2nd place at Watkins Glen, 1993

Wally Dallenbach

Wally Dallenbach is back! After a disappointing half-season in '94 as Richard Petty's driver, and then sitting out the '95 season, Wally showed up at the season-opening Daytona 500 in Bud Moore's unsponsored #15 T-Bird. The plain white car without any decals was very easy to spot because it was right up front, running 2nd and 3rd for quite a few laps. Before the race was halfway over, the veteran Bud Moore had secured a sponsor to run for the rest of the season. Near the end, Wally got "freight-trained" out of what would have been a top-five finish. He still finished in the top ten and is off to a great start for '96.

This son of a former USAC star is one to watch. Welcome back, Wally.

Hometown: Basalt, CO • **Birthday:** 5/23/63
Family: Robin, Jacob, Wyatt • **Car:** Team Bud Moore #15 Ford
Fan Club: N/A

Dale Earnhardt

Career Highlights

- Tied Richard Petty's record of seven Winston Cup championships, 1994

- Won over $3 million, 1994

- 69 Winston Cup wins

- Won over $25 million in career

Dale Earnhardt

"You win some, you lose some, you wreck some."
Dale Earnhardt

Then you win some more. Then you catch up with The King. Then you position yourself to break The King's record. But to put it all in perspective, Dale says, "I may share the title with Richard, but he'll always be 'The King.'" And Dale will always be Dale, which means he'll give credit to his entire team at Richard Childress racing: "The chemistry is there, you don't have to tell each other what to do, you just do it." And they sure have.

Any more goals? Dale plans to race through the turn of the century. He'll be 50 in the year 2002. Everyone knows an eighth Winston Cup title is in his sights. And perhaps that elusive Daytona 500 will finally become a reality before he climbs out the window for the last time. But if it never does, the name Earnhardt is firmly positioned in the record book for all time. Somewhere, Ralph Earnhardt, the former short track charger, is mighty proud, mighty proud.

Hometown: Kannapolis, NC • **Birthday:** 4/29/52
Family: Teresa, Kerry, Kelly King, Ralph Dale, Jr., Taylor Nicole • **Car:** #3 Chevy Goodwrench
Fan Club: 5301-A West W.T. Harris Blvd., Charlotte, NC 28269

Bill Elliott

Career Highlights

- Won 40 Winston Cup races

- Won Daytona 500, 1985

- Voted Most Popular Driver by fans 9 times

Bill Elliott

Whoever said you can't go home again hasn't talked to Bill Elliott. After a long absence, he's rejoining his brothers Ernie and Dan, who played a big role in his early success. Together with car dealer Charles Hardy, they will be campaigning in the #94 McDonald's Ford Thunderbird. Coca Cola is also a major sponsor.

Bill will soon be in his 21st year of Winston Cup racing. The fans have voted him the most popular driver 9 times. Here's maybe one reason for that vote: The number #94 is the number his nephew Casey had planned to use as a driver before he became terminally ill. Way to go Bill . . . totally awesome.

Hometown: Dawsonville, GA • **Birthday:** 10/8/55
Family: Cindy, Starr • **Car:** #94 McDonald's Ford
Fan Club: P.O. Box 248, Dawsonville, GA 30534

Jeff Gordon

Career Highlights

- Won Inaugural Brick-yard 400, 1994

- Upset the applecart by winning championship, 1995

- Fastest rising star in NASCAR

Jeff Gordon

"Flash" Gordon has certainly lived up to his nickname, and the potential that Rick Hendrick spotted in him has proved itself. NASCAR fans are seeing the beginnings of a legend like I haven't seen since the early 60's and car #43. And NASCAR's veteran drivers are seeing Gordon's rear bumper all too frequently.

This kid who seemingly came out of nowhere got an early start and was driving sprint cars and winning when most kids his age were still pedaling bikes. Yes, the future looks mighty bright for the kid in the #24 car. Caution . . . wear your shades as he flashes by.

Hometown: Pittsboro, IN ● **Birthday:** 8/4/71
Family: Brooke ● **Car:** #24 Dupont Chevy
Fan Club: P.O. Box 515, Williams, AZ 86046-0515

Steve Grissom

Career Highlights

- Finished 2nd to Jeff Burton in Rookie of the Year, 1994

- Back-to-back top ten finishes at Richmond & Dover

- Won over $300,000 in first full year in Winston Cup racing

Steve Grissom

Another of the new kids on the track, Steve is showing up in the front a lot. With Buddy Parrot as his crew chief, expect to see him in the winner's circle soon. Buddy has worked with Roger Penske and Rusty Wallace; the man knows how to win.

Like most rookies, Grissom's first year had its highs and lows. Potential-showing finishes at Talledega, Richmond and Dover were tempered by failing to qualify at Daytona and the Brickyard. All part of a racer's life, and Steve has shown he's in it for the long haul. Steve came to Winston from the Busch circuit where he was the champion in 1993.

Hometown: Gadsen, Alabama • Birthday 6/26/63
Family: Susan • **Car:** #29 Meinke Chevy
Fan Club: 23110 S.R. 54 No. 198, Lutz, FL 33549

Bobby Hamilton

Career Highlights

- Rookie of the Year, 1991

- Picked to drive for "The King," 1995

- Won over $2 million in career

Bobby Hamilton

Though it's been too long since the Petty blue 43 has visited the winner's circle, the pressure on anyone who takes the wheel of this machine has to be something else again. The honor is one that few have had the opportunity to share.

Bobby is the 5th driver in three years to get that chance. Obviously both Bobby and Richard feel he can get the job done or he would not be sitting in that seat. Times have changed but one thing is for certain: Petty knows how to win, and he will figure out a way to do it with someone else driving. Bobby, I wish you the best; after all, that's my old number, too, you're runnin' with.

Hometown: Nashville, TN • **Birthday:** 9/29/57
Family: Debbie, Bobby Jr. • **Car:** #43 STP Pontiac
Fan Club: N/A

Ernie Irvan

Career Highlights

- Daytona 500 winner, 1991

- Won over $5.5 million in career

Ernie Irvan

Ernie's accident has sidelined him for awhile, but the man is back. If anyone can do it, it's Ernie. In just 6 years of Winston competition, he has proven himself to be a big winner and was in contention for the championship when he crashed.

Ernie stays a hard charger as he continues where he left off. The outpouring of support from the fans and everyone associated with racing had to help. He sure has started off '96 with a bang by capturing the outside pole at Daytona.

Hometown: Salinas, CA • Birthday 1/13/1959
Family: Kim, Jordan • **Car:** #28 Texaco Ford
Fan Club: 1027 Central Dr., Concord, NC 28027

Dale Jarrett

Career Highlights

- Daytona 500 winner, 1993 and 1996

- Won over $5 million in career

- Son of NASCAR legend Ned Jarrett

Dale Jarrett

The thing I'll always remember the most about Dale's career is the day his dad was covering the Daytona 500 in the broadcast booth, when he realized his son was going to win the big one. Ned, who is generally calm and very fair as a reporter, lost control, and deservedly so. In doing so he let the rest of the world in on the excitement a driver feels when taking a race.

Stepping in for Ernie Irvan in the #28 car, Dale has high hopes for all at Robert Yates racing, which has endured far too much bad luck the last few years. If he can find a way to add some of Ned's excitement from that day in 1993 to the fuel tank without getting caught . . . well, anything could happen.

Hometown: Concord NC • **Birthday:** 11/26/56
Family: Kelly, Jason, Natalee, Karsyn, Zachary • **Car:** #88 Quality Care Ford
Fan Club: Box 564, Conover, NC 28613

Bobby Labonte

Career Highlights

- Won Coca-Cola 600 for first Winston Cup win, 1995

- Second Winston Cup win followed 2 weeks later at the Genuine Draft 400 in Michigan

Bobby Labonte

In the weird course of life, Bobby lines up alphabetically behind Ernie Irvan and Dale Jarrett. All three have been affected by Ernie's crash. Bobby took over for Dale as Dale took over for Ernie and the cars and the world go round and round.

After a wild and wooly ride in '94 that included an emergency crash landing in a plane, Bobby is doing very well, with his first three Winston wins driving for Joe Gibbs, former Super Bowl-winning football coach and owner of a Daytona 500 win. In just a few years of full-time Winston competition, Bobby has added his name to the list of contenders.

Hometown: Corpus Christi, Texas • **Birthday:** 5/8/64
Family: Donna, Robert Tyler • **Car:** #18 Interstate Chevy
Fan Club: P.O. Box 358, Trinity, NC 27370

Terry Labonte

Career Highlights

- Daytona 500 winner, 1990

- Passed his 500th Winston start in 1995 with over 16 wins and 350 top tens

Terry Labonte

Some guys just go quietly about their work. As steady and reliable as his sponsor Kellogg's Corn Flakes, Terry has been there since 1978, and has run a full Winston schedule since 1979. Two thirds of the time he has finished in the top ten. That's being consistent!

That consistency carried Terry to the Winston Cup Championship in 1984, and perhaps with the backing of the Rick Hendrick organization, it will take him there again.

1995 proved to be one of those years, as Terry aced three wins and 14 top 5's plus 17 top 10 finishes. His career earnings are over $10 million. Rick Hendrick has demonstrated that he has the eye for talent, and adding Terry to his teams of contenders has certainly proved a wise move.

Hometown: Corpus Christi, TX • **Birthday:** 11/16/56
Family: Kim, Justin, Kelly • **Car:** #5 Kellogg's Chevy
Fan Club: P.O. Box 4617, Archdale, NC 27263

Dave Marcis

Career Highlights

- Celebrating his 29th year of Winston Cup Competition

- Won over $4 million in career

Dave Marcis

Like Harry Gant and Darrell Waltrip, Dave Marcis has been around and around and around. He is nearing start #800 and has no plans to let up on the gas. One of the last of the independents, Dave is jack of all trades in his racing organization. He finds the sponsor, works on the car, and drives it on Sunday or Saturday or whenever there is a race.

In 1975 he was runner up to Richard Petty in the points chase. Unlike most of the drivers, Dave has been driving for himself for all but 4 years. I think he prefers it even though there is a definite advantage to having someone else worry about the bills. But then Dave is the boss.

Hometown: Wausau, WI • **Birthday:** 3/1/41
Family: Helen, Shawn Marie, Richard • **Car:** #71 Chevy Lumina
Fan Club: N/A

Sterling Marlin

Career Highlights

- Won back-to-back Daytona 500's, 1994 and 1995

- Won many pole positions including Daytona, Talladega, and Darlington

- NASCAR's Rookie of the Year, 1983

- Won Track Championships at Nashville Raceway three consecutive years, 1980-82

- Won over $7,000,000

Sterling Marlin

If at first you don't succeed, try, try again. That old saying will probably never be illustrated better in stock car racing history as well as it has been by Sterling Marlin. And his reward for his refusal to give up? None other than the grand prize in the world of stock car racing. The Daytona 500, a race that some Winston Cup champions have never won. And if that weren't enough, he did it again the next year, putting himself in the very elite class of back-to-back Daytona winners. Why, I'm sure more than one driver would trade a double Darlington or a triple Talledega for just one of Sterling's rides to the winner's circle at Daytona.

This good-natured Tennessee farm boy learned his craft by working on the pit crew of his father Coo Coo's team. He learned well, too. He started driving in 1976, and was running in the big leagues by 1978. At the Nashville Raceway he was a multi-time track champion like his daddy, and NASCAR's Rookie of the Year in 1983.

Sterling ran well in points battle for 1995 and almost won it all. He has a good chance to be the Winston Champion very soon if he hangs in there. I'd doubt he knows any other way.

Hometown: Columbia, TN • **Birthday:** 6/30/57
Family: Paula, Steadman, Sutherlin • **Car:** #4 Kodak Chevrolet
Fan Club: 1116 W. 7th St., Suite 62, Columbia, TN 38401

Mark Martin

Career Highlights

- Won over \$10 million in Winston Cup career

- Mounted serious challenges for the Winston Cup title for last several years. Was second in 1994.

Mark Martin

Racing luck, that quicksilver concoction that no one can put their finger on, has a way of upsetting the steadiest applecart. No matter how well you build and prepare a car, you never know what's waiting around the next turn. Sometimes it's running out of fuel at the Daytona 500 or having a tire go down with just a few laps to go.

Mark has had his share of luck, both good and bad. The nine years that he has run for Jack Roush, though, have been pretty good as he finds himself in contention for the cup again this year. With seemingly more contenders than in many a year, it just might come down to a little racing luck. Unlike his likeness on the facing page, Mark usually wears his lucky grin, and that might do the trick.

Hometown: Batesville, AR • **Birthday:** 1/9/59
Family: Arlene, Heather, Rachel, Stacy, Matthew Clyde
Car: #6 Valvoline Ford • **Fan Club:** P.O. Box 68, Ash Flat, AR 72513

Rick Mast

Career Highlights

- Won almost $3 million in 5 years of full-time Winston Cup Competition

- Won pole for the first Brickyard 400, 1994

Rick Mast

Like the number it carries, Rick's car has been #1 at the start of a race or seriously challenged for the lead many times. Winding up in first at the end has been just a little more of a problem, but the team is working at it.

Winning the pole at the first Brickyard 400 had to be a confidence builder as 70 drivers tried to unseat him. He had a hard-fought battle with Dale Earnhardt at Rockingham in 1994. One second separated the two. But it should not be long before the #1 takes its first ride to the winner's circle with Mr. Mast at the wheel.

Hometown: Rockridge Baths, VA • **Birthday:** 3/4/57
Family: Sharon, Ricky • **Car:** #1 Precision Ford
Fan Club: N/A

Jeremy Mayfield

Career Highlights

- Hired by Cale Yarborough in his first full season, 1994

- ARCA Rookie of the Year, 1993

Jeremy Mayfield

Owensboro, Kentucky is one of those small Southern towns with a big distinction when it comes to stock car racing. Perhaps it was Darrell Waltrip's doing; he's from there. As is Darrell's brother Michael, and David and Jeff Green, and Jeremy Mayfield. That's a lot of professional drivers from one small town.

It might be small but it's not slow, and neither is Jeremy's start in Winston Cup racing. Coming off of eight top 5 finishes in the ARCA series, he ran solid in the middle of the pack for the '94 Winston season despite driving for three teams. With three-time consecutive champ Cale Yarborough's guidance, Jeremy has a strong future in front of him.

Hometown: Owensboro, KY • **Birthday:** 5/27/69
Family: Christina • **Car:** #98 RCA Ford
Fan Club: P.O. Box 1329, Providence, RI 02903

Ted Musgrave

Career Highlights

- Won 3 pole positions in 1994, all in Virginia

- Finished 7th in points, 1995

- Won $3 million in career

Ted Musgrave

Hooking up with the Jack Roush Team seems to be the right thing for both Ted and Jack. Both the team and driver have steadily shown big improvement. In their third year together Ted has seven top-five finishes in the Family Channel Ford.

Ted has won poles on the shorter tracks at Richmond and Virginia. A few bad breaks (like a timing chain) prevented a higher than 13th place in '94 points race. Halfway through the '95 season found Ted in 4th nipping at the bumpers of Dale Earnhardt, Sterling Marlin, and Jeff Gordon. For the '96 season, as they say at the Family Channel, "Stay tuned and watch!"

Hometown: Franklin, WI • **Birthday:** 12/18/55
Family: Deb, Teddy Jr., Justin, Brittany Nicole • **Car:** #16 Family Channel Ford
Fan Club: P.O. Box 1089, Liberty, NC 27298

Joe Nemechek

Career Highlights

- Won pole in 1994 Winston Select, finished 10th place

- BUSCH champion, 1992

Joe Nemechek

Unlike the Polish victory lap popularized by the late champion Alan Kulwicki, Joe seems to know how to advance around a track quickly. The 1992 Busch champion has made some strong moves in his first two years at Winston Cup racing. Besides winning a pole, he has qualified up front at several races in '94 and '95.

The Big Move came in '95, though, as Joe announced the formation of his own team with Tony Furr, who was chief wrench for Greg Sacks. For most rookies, just settling down with driving chores in the Winston is a BIG job. For Joe it's just part of it, as he looks to take his first victory lap . . . Polish or otherwise.

Hometown: Lakeland, FL • **Birthday:** 9/26/63
Family: Andrea • **Car:** #87 Burger King Chevy
Fan Club: P.O. Box 1131, Mooresville, NC 28115

Kyle Petty

Career Highlights

- Third-generation driver of most famous name in Stock Car Racing

- 8 career wins and over $7 million in earnings

Kyle Petty

In my book, *Long Ride on a Short Track*, I got to interview several drivers whose fathers were short track heroes. So even though I've only met Kyle briefly when he was promoting his book, *Kyle at 200 MPH*, I can get an idea of what pressures must have been on him when he first started out in the late '70's. The fact that we're both musicians and that I drove gives me a bit more insight also. However, I don't think anyone but Kyle will ever know what it feels like to be Richard Petty's son and Lee Petty's grandson. In spite of that, my helmet's off to Kyle because he has shown the racing world that he is truly his own man.

After a poor 15th season where he placed 15th in the points, a new sponsor and a recommitment with car owner Felix Sabates has already led to a trip to victory lane. You can bet there'll be more.

Hometown: Randleman, NC • **Birthday:** 6/2/60
Family: Patti, Adam, Austin, Montgomery • **Car:** #42 Coors Pontiac
Fan Club: 8318 Pineville-Matthews Rd., Ste. 708-116, Charlotte, NC 28273

Ricky Rudd

Career Highlights

- Realized his goal of owner/driver, 1994

- Visited Victory Lane for 13 consecutive years

Ricky Rudd

Starting your own team can often be an exercise in frustration, especially when you have to do the driving. Well, Ricky did it in 1994 and I don't think he has any regrets. His first four races found him in the top ten at the end and it got better from there. Up at Loudon, New Hampshire, during the Slick 50, Ricky went fender to fender with Dale Earnhardt to score the new team's first victory.

A family man, he missed qualifying at Bristol to be at his wife's side for the birth of their son Landon. He wound up 5th in the points race in his first year, which is truly spectacular. Driving a Ford in a year of the Monte Carlo he had one win and 10 top-five and 16 top-10 finishes.

Hometown: Chesapeake, VA • **Birthday:** 9/12/56
Family: Linda, Landon • **Car:** #10 Tide Ford
Fan Club: P.O. Box 7586, Richmond, VA 23231

Ken Schrader

Career Highlights

- Daytona 500 Winner, 1989

- Won over $7 million in career

Ken Schrader

As NASCAR's 1985 Rookie of the Year completes his first decade of Winston Cup competition, Kenny has plenty to reflect on and lots to look forward too. With well over 300 races behind him, he had his best showing so far in the points battle of '94 when he finished 4th.

Driving for one of Rick Hendrick's three teams, Ken is always consistent and now with BUD his hometown sponsor, Ken Howes as his crew chief, and "Papa Joe" Hendrick's organization and '95's hard luck behind him, the next decade is looking just as good if not better.

Hometown: Fenton, MO • **Birthday:** 5/29/55
Family: Ann, Dorothy, Sheldon • **Car:** #25 Budweiser Chevy
Fan Club: P.O. Box 599, Licking, MO 65542

Morgan Shepherd

Career Highlights

- Won over $1 million in 1994, the best year of his long career

- NASCAR Sportsman Champion, 1980

Morgan Shepherd

After driving for the Wood Brothers, one of the most famous teams in NASCAR history, Morgan is in a new deal for '96. He is rejoining Butch Mock, whom he ran for in the 80's.

1994 marked his most successful year yet. As he nears the end of a quarter century of Winston competition, another victory would break Harry Gant's record as the oldest driver to win a Winston. With his experience, don't be surprised when it happens.

Hometown: Conover, NC • **Birthday:** 10/12/41
Family: Cindy, Debbie, Crystal, Terri, Cynthia Morgan Jr., Shanda Renee
Car: #75 Remington Ford • **Fan Club:** P.O. Box 1456, Stow, OH 44224

Jimmy Spencer

Career Highlights

- First win came at Daytona Firecracker, 1994

- Followed up at Talledega 3 weeks later

Jimmy Spencer

Modifieds, NASCAR's oldest division, has often provided its most exciting moments, as these low-slung, fat-tired, 700 hp hot rods battle each other on the short tracks across the country. Winston drivers who came from the modified division include the Bodines, Greg Sacks, and most recently Jimmy Spencer, a.k.a. "Mr. Excitement."

Jimmy has been given that handle by fans and drivers as he contributes to some high anxiety on the super speedways. He drives on them almost the same as he does on a short track. The fact that he still competes occasionally in a Modified seems to add to that excitement.

Hometown: Berwick, PA • **Birthday:** 2/15/57
Family: Pat, Jimmy, Katrina • **Car:** #23 Smokin Joe's Ford
Fan Club: P.O. Box 1626, Mooresville, NC 28115

Hut Stricklin

Career Highlights

- Almost 200 starts and over $2 million in winnings

- Former Goody's Dash Champion, 1986

Hut Stricklin

Hut's been close to that first Winston checker. Real close, such as when he was driving for Bobby Allison in 1991 and came in second in the Miller Draft 400. But like many of his peers he knows how tough it is to grab one. That's what drives these guys: this ain't no Sunday drive.

Hut has also driven for Junior Johnson, in the McDonald's Ford during 1993, and Travis Carter in the newly formed Smokin Joe's team. Mid-season of '95 they announced that they would part, and now Hut turns the wheel for Kenny Berenstien in the seat that was briefly occupied by sprint car champ Steve Kinser. Just like chassis adjustments—working step by step to get the right combo—the team of driver, car, owner, and crew takes a lot of fine tuning to produce a winner.

Hometown: Calera, AL • **Birthday:** 6/24/61
Family: Pam, Taylor Lane, Tabitha Jean • **Car:** #8 Stavola Bros. Ford
Fan Club: P.O. Box 1080, Calera, AL 35040

Dick Trickle

Career Highlights

- Won over \$2 million in career

- NASCAR Rookie of the Year, 1989

Dick Trickle

Patience in the racing game almost contradicts the nature of the sport: to be faster than the other guy. But like speed, without patience you can't win a race. You also can't win without the right combination of driver, car, and team. Need proof? Ask Sterling Marlin.

Patience may be about to pay off for Dick Trickle, as well. He is a short track legend in the Midwest who has run limited campaigns in Winston, starting in 1970. In that year, he entered his own car in Daytona and finished 10 places higher than his starting position. Since '89, he has run a full schedule with the Cale Yarborough, Stavola, Rahmoc, and Moore teams. He is going for a new team (TBA) for 1996.

Hometown: Wisconsin Rapids, WI • **Birthday:** 10/27/41
Family: Darlene, Victoria, Todd, Chad • **Car:** TBA
Fan Club: 5415 Vesuvius-Furnace Rd., Iron Station, NC 28080

Kenny Wallace

Career Highlights

- NASCAR's Busch Series 1989 Rookie of the Year

- Runner-up, Busch Cup, 1991

- 4th in Goody's 500, 1994

Kenny Wallace

Lady Luck, a mascot long associated with auto racing, can run with you or against you. When she turned mean and nasty on Ernie Irvan in 1994 she winked at Kenny Wallace. Kenny was called up from the Busch Grand National circuit by Robert Yates to fill in for Ernie after his terrible crash. Kenny did a credible job for the #28 team and finished out the rest of his Busch tour, too. His strongest showing was at Martinsville where he finished 4th.

Kenny's strong performance in '94 may have led car owner Fil Martucci to decide to move his team up into Winston Cup competition for '95, where Kenny took the wheel of #81 TIC Ford. The youngest brother of drivers Mike and Rusty, Kenny worked his way through the ranks of the ASA in the midwest and the NASCAR Busch circuit, being voted Rookie of the Year on both circuits. His first run in the Winston series placed him in third place of the rookies of 1993. That year he drove for Felix Sabates in the Dirt Devil car. Whatever Lady Luck has in store for Kenny, you know he's ready and able to handle it.

Hometown: St. Louis, MO • **Birthday:** 8/23/63
Family: Kim, Brooke, Brandy, Brittany • **Car:** #81 TIC Ford
Fan Club: P.O. Box 3050, Concord, NC 28025

Mike Wallace

Career Highlights

- After 34th place start at Atlanta in 1994, led race twice

- Won over 300 Short Track events in Midwest

Mike Wallace

Breaks. You need them on and off the track. The off-track break Mike Wallace needed came when Bobby Hillen left the Junie Donlaveys team. Mike got the ride and finished fifth at the Atlanta Hooters 500. He also led that race at one point.

But like most seasons with a new driver and team, there are hills and valleys, good breaks, and bad breaks, while everyone tries to sort it out and find the way to the checkered flag. Failing to qualify for several races is a hard dose of reality in today's racing game where sometimes one mph can shut you out. But Mike didn't win all those other races, including a Mid-America region championship, on breaks alone. That's why he is where he is, in Winston Cup, and when it all comes together, look for him in victory lane.

Hometown: St. Louis, MO • **Birthday:** 3/10/59
Family: Carla, Lindsey, Christina • **Car:** #90 Helig-Meyers Ford
Fan Club: 224 Rolling Hill Rd., Suite 9A, Mooresville, NC 28115

Rusty Wallace

Career Highlights

- Winston Cup
  champion, 1989

- Won over $12 million
  in career

Rusty Wallace

The same breaks that affect his brothers Kenny and Mike also affect Rusty as he looks for a way to nail another Winston Cup title down. He's been so close more than once, including riding Dale Earnhardt's bumper twice as the breaks worked for and against him.

The one thing the team does not lack is desire. His pit crew (the fastest on the circuit) is just one shining example, as is Rusty's record 40 Winston wins. In fact, he has led in wins several times and still lost the points race, further underscoring how important luck can be in racing.

Hometown: St. Louis, MO • **Birthday:** 8/14/56
Family: Patti, Greg, Katie, Stephen • **Car:** #2 Miller Ford
Fan Club: 224 Rolling Hills Rd., Suite 5A, Mooresville, NC 28115

Darrell Waltrip

Career Highlights

- 3-Time WInston Cup champion

- Third place in all-time wins with 84; tied with Bobby Allison

- Won over $14 million in career

Darrell Waltrip

It's amazing that anyone can achieve all that Darrell has in his 23-year career and still find goals to strive for. But that's what makes this guy Darrell Waltrip tick. He is as determined as a rookie to add another notch to his belt to prove something to both himself and his fans.

He has shaken up his team to help achieve those goals, and the results seem to be working, including four top-five and eight top-10 finishes in the '95 season. His goal is to have 100 wins and one more championship before retirement.

Hometown: Franklin , TN • **Birthday:** 2/5/47
Family: Stevie, Jessica Leigh, Sarah • **Car:** #17 Western Auto Chevy
Fan Club: P.O. Box 855, Franklin, TN 37065

Michael Waltrip

Career Highlights

- Won over $4 million in career

- Starting 11th season

- NASCAR Dash champion, 1983

Michael Waltrip

How tough is it to win a Winston Cup Race? Well, of the 150-odd winners since it began in 1949, one third of them have only won once. And for some of them it took almost twenty years to do that.

Having a big brother that's only two notches below the King in all-time wins does not by itself get you into that club. But coming off his best season yet Michael is poised to notch his belt for the first time. He had two 2nd's last year, and a 2nd is just split seconds away from a 1st.

Hometown: Owensboro, KY • **Birthday:** 4/30/63
Family: Elizabeth • **Car:** #21 Citgo Ford
Fan Club: P.O. Box 339, Sherrills Ford, NC 28673

Bobby Allison

Living Legend of Stock Car Racing

Career Highlights

- 3rd overall winningest driver with 84 career Winston Cup victories; tied with Darrell Waltrip

- 2-time Modified Champion, 1964 and 1965

- Began driving in late 1950's and ended with a crash at Pocono in 1988

Bobby Allison

Islip Speedway in Islip, Long Island, has been gone since 1984, but the echoes of the exhausts of Petty, Johnson, Jarrett, Scott, and many more NASCAR Southern Boys still mingle across the property with all the local legends. One of the first to mingle with us was a young Florida feller named Bob Allison. He used to tow his little cut-down '36 Chevy #312 there weekly all alone. We had a 500-lapper there and Bobby took a second behind local superstar Jimmy Hendrickson. The most famous incident at Islip was when the longstanding feud between Petty & Allison erupted there in 1968 with a hilarious outcome. It's retold in great detail by Richard & Bobby in the video "The Bobby Allison Story." An amazing man with an amazing story, say hello to him you'll be glad you did.

Ned Jarrett

Living Legend of Stock Car Racing

Career Highlights

- 7th overall winningest driver with 50 career Winston Cup victories; tied with Junior Johnson

- 2 Winston Cup championships, 1961 and 1965

- Retired in 1967 to begin his new career as NASCAR's most popular broadcaster

Ned Jarrett

On Dale Jarrett's page I recall how excited Ned got as he broadcast his son winning the 1993 Daytona 500. They say during the replay he was just as excited and the others in the booth had to remind him it's OK and to calm down because Dale had already won it.

Normally a calm and knowledgeable broadcaster, I remember seeing Ned drive his number 11 Ford with hardly a decal on it in 1965, the year he won the Championship. He was all business, steady as she goes. Ned had a great career in the car and is tied with Junior Johnson at 7th in all time wins at 50. I always enjoy listening to his broadcasts as they are as insightful as you can get, and when Dale is out there leading Ned, puts it to the floor.

Junior Johnson

Living Legend of Stock Car Racing

Career Highlights

- 7th overall winningest driver with 50 career Winston Cup victories; tied with Ned Jarrett

- 1975 movie "Last American Hero" based on his life

- Most successful team owner in NASCAR history

- Raced from 1953 - 1966

Junior Johnson

It was 1965 at Islip Speedway, a 1/5 mile oval up north where the Southern Stars were all runnin' in second gear: Petty, Jarrett, Panch, and Junior in his 427 Chevy. Going close to 90, Junior's throttle stuck and he sailed over the wall and out into the parking lot. The original Mr. Excitement.

Until '95, this "Last American Hero" kept going flat out and fielded some of the most exciting teams in Winston Cup. In fact, it was Junior who got R.J. Reynolds involved with NASCAR, and Grand National racing became Winston Cup. Another of Junior's many accomplishments was he "discovered" the draft in 1960 at Daytona and it helped him win it. Big doings from a big man, but you should have seen him go over the wall at Islip . . . the locals had never seen anything like it!

Richard Petty

Living Legend of Stock Car Racing

Career Highlights

- 1st overall winningest driver with 200 Winston Cup victories; a record considered unbeatable

- 7 Winston Cup championships

- Stock Car Racing's greatest ambassador

- Raced from 1958 - 1993

Richard Petty

The King

I was 15 years old the first time I saw Richard drive. It was on the Bridgehampton, Long Island, road course. He was simply amazing as he kept that Plymouth on the track as most of his competitors, like Fireball Roberts, Joe Weatherly, and Rex White, were barreling all over it. I can still recall the screech of tires as they came out of the hairpin turn that led onto the main straight. You could not see them from the grandstand till they were on the straight. Many came out backwards, but young Richard just motored on. I was in the process of building my first stock car then for our local track. It was a 1937 Plymouth sportsman class. I didn't have a number picked out till that day. Yep . . . I lettered #43 on my door when the KING was still a prince!

Cale Yarborough

Living Legend of Stock Car Racing

Career Highlights

- 3 back-to-back Winston Cup championships, 1976-1978; only driver ever to do so

- 4th overall winningest driver with 83 Winston Cup victories

- Raced from 1957 - 1989

Cale Yarborough

A few select drivers have won more than one Winston Cup Championship, but only one has done it three times in a row. From 1976 to 1978 Cale owned the Cup. During his career, he put 83 Winston victories in the record book. That means Dale Earnhardt has to win 19 more to tie Cale for 5th in all time wins.

Today Cale fields the #98 RCA Ford with Jeremy Mayfield at the wheel. Some of the folks who have driven for him include Dale Jarrett, Dick Trickle, Lake Speed, Chuck Bown, Jimmy Hensley, Chad Little, Bobby Hillin, and Derrick Cope.

Atlanta Motor Speedway

Track Facts

Length: 1.522 miles

Banks: 24°

Records: Qual: 185.830 mph
Greg Sacks, 1984

Race: 156.849 mph
Dale Earnhardt, 1990

Schedule: Purolator 500, March
NAPA 500, November

Tickets: P.O. Box 500, Hampton, GA 30228
404-946-4211

Atlanta Motor Speedway

With two swooping 1/2-mile turns connected by two 1/4-mile dragstrip straights, Atlanta is one fast racetrack. Greg Sacks set the record there after it was repaved recently at over 185. It boasts the best view of any track on the circuit and also offers a 2.5-mile road course. The view from the infield is as good as it is in the grandstand. Plans are underway to increase seating to over 225,000. It is located just south of Atlanta on Highways 19 and 41.

Bristol International Raceway

Track Facts

Length: 1.5 miles

Banks: 36°

Records: Qual: 124.946 mph
Chuck Bown, 4/94

Race: 101.074 mph
Charlie Glotzbach, 1971

Schedule: Food City 500, April
Goodys 500, August

Tickets: P.O. Box 3966 Bristol, TN 37625
423-764-1161

Bristol International Raceway

Located in northeast Tennessee near the border of Virginia, Bristol is the little track with the big banks. At 36 degrees, its like a motordrome. It's very hard on drivers and equipment. It is also the site of Winston Cup's oldest night race. Future plans include expanding the seating and a 250-suite building.

Charlotte Motor Speedway

Track Facts

Length: 1.5 miles

Banks: 24°

Records: Qual: 185.759 mph
Ward Burton, 10/94

Race: 145.504 mph
Dale Earnhardt, 5/93

Schedule: Winston Select, May
Goody's Pole Night, May
Coca Cola 600, May
Winston Pole Night, October
UAW-GN 500, October

Tickets: P.O. Box 600, Concord, NC 28026
704-455-3200

Humpy Wheeler, who started his career selling hot dogs to the folks who came to see the good ol' boys hot dog around in the dirt, has really gone uptown at Charlotte. Like Bill France, Humpy is a visionary and has promoted stock car racing in the biggest ways imaginable, like offering condos at a race track and selling them on the Tonight Show with Johnny Carson. Running year-round entertainment and four Winston events per year, Charlotte Motor Speedway sets the standard in SUPER superspeedways.

Darlington Raceway

Track Facts

Length: 1.366 miles

Banks: 23° and 25°

Records: Qual: 166.998 mph
9/94

Race: 139.958 mph
3/93

Schedule: TranSouth Financial 400, March
Mountain Dew Southern 500, September

Tickets: P.O. Box 500, Darlington, SC 29532
803-395-8499

Darlington Raceway

Darlington has been letting drivers earn their stripes since 1950 on the oldest superspeedway on the NASCAR circuit. Billed as the track "Too Tough to Tame" and the "Lady in Black," Darlington is growing into the future with new suites and grandstands that make it a true historic showplace. Veteran Jim Hunter is the President and General Manager. Russell Braham handles PR, and Karen Belk hospitality.

Daytona

Track Facts

Length: 2.5 miles

Banks: 31°

Records: Qual: 210.364 mph
Bill Elliott, 1987

Race: 177.602 mph (Daytona 500)
Buddy Baker, 1980

173.473 mph (Pepsi 400)
Bobby Allison, 1980

Schedule: Daytona 500, February
Pepsi 400, July

Tickets: P.O. Box 2801, Daytona Beach, FL
32120, 904-253-7223

Daytona

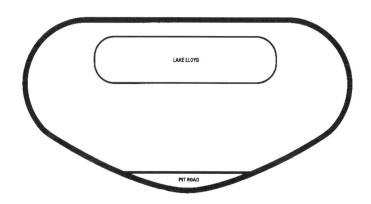

LAKE LLOYD

PIT ROAD

Home of NASCAR

They may build bigger tracks, they may build faster tracks, but they'll never build another DAYTONA, Bill France Sr.'s technicolor dream come true. It was constructed in the late 1950's after Bill realized that racing halfway down the beach, then returning on a two-lane blacktop, wasn't gonna get it. Daytona is like The King; say it and it means . . . STOCK CAR RACING!

Dover Downs

Track Facts

Length: 1 mile

Banks: 24°

Records: Qual: 152.840 mph
Geoff Bodine, 9/94

Race: 125.945 mph
Bill Elliott, 9/90

Schedule: Budweiser 500, June
Splitfire Spark Plug 500, September

Tickets: P.O. Box 843, Dover, DE 19903
800-441-RACE

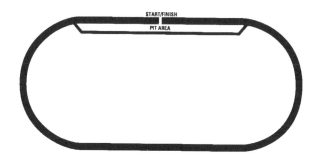

When Dover was first built, Modified legend Fred Harbach drove his '35 Chevy coach around the "Monster Mile" at 134+ mph. He said he was NEVER on a bank like that. With its new concrete surface (the only one in NASCAR), Dover is still providing thrills a quarter-century later for both driver and spectator. It seats over 100,000 and hosts both the opening and closing events in the Winston Northeast tour. Denis McGlynn, Gerald Dunning, and Al Robinson are the managers.

Indianapolis Motor Speedway

Track Facts

Length: 2.5 miles

Banks: 9-12°

Records: Qual: 172.414 mph
Rick Mast, 8/94

Race: 131.977 mph
Jeff Gordon, 8/94

Schedule: Brickyard 400, August

Tickets: P.O. Box 24910, Speedway, IN
46224, 317-484-6700

Indianapolis Motor Speedway

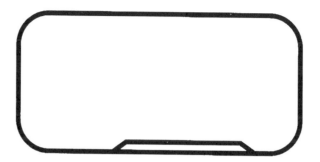

The oldest and most famous speedway in the U.S. became the newest on the Winston tour when in 1994 STOCK CARS rumbled over the 2.5 mile once-brick-paved course for the first time. An Indiana native and new Winston driver Jeff Gordon drove into racing history by capturing the checker in front of the largest crowd to ever witness a Winston race. An estimated 250,000 enthusiastic race fans were on hand. Hey Indy, what took ya so long?

Track Facts

Length: .526 mile

Banks: 12°

Records: Qual: 94.185 mph
Ted Musgrave, 9/94

Race: 79.185 mph
Cale Yarborough, 9/78

Schedule: Hanes 500, April
Goody's 500, September

Tickets: P.O. Box 3311, Martinsville, VA
24115, 703-956-3151

Martinsville Speedway

START | FINISH
PIT AREA
PIT AREA

Clay Earles built his 1/2-mile track in 1947 two years before NASCAR held it's first race. Bill France paid Clay a visit and it became one of the original tracks on the fledgling NASCAR circuit. Against all kinds of advice Clay paved it in 1955. It thrived, and has become widely known for its comfort and action. It's fairly flat and is the shortest track on the circuit. Clay Campbell is the general manager.

Michigan International Speedway

Track Facts

Length: 2 miles

Banks: 18°

Records: Qual: 181.082 mph
Geoff Bodine, 8/94

Race: 160.912 mph
Davey Allison, 6/91

Schedule: Miller Genuine Draft 400, June
Goodwrench 400, August

Tickets: 12626 U.S. 12, Brooklyn, MI 49230
800-354-1010

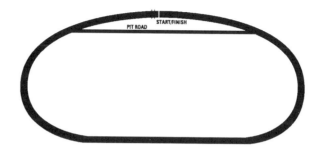

Its WIDE, its HIGH, and its FAST. Geoff Bodine got around it in under 40 seconds. At two miles long, that's hauling. With an outstanding view of the entire track and cars going three and four wide at 180+ mph, it's no wonder it's rapidly approaching it's 30th anniversary. Gene Haskett and Bill Miller keep it running smoothly, and they are always upgrading the facility. It's tracks like this that will ensure the growth of Stock Car Racing well into the next century.

Track Facts

Length: 1.058 miles

Banks: 12°

Records: Qual: 127.197 mph
Ernie Irvan, 7/94

Race: 105.947 mph
Rusty Wallace, 7/93

Schedule: Slick 50, July

Tickets: P.O. Box 7888, Loudon, NH 03301
603-783-4931

Over 72,000 race fans showed up at Loudon, NH, to watch the 2nd annual Slick 50, making it New England's largest sporting event. Long a hotbed of stock car racing, Loudon also hosts Busch and Featherlite Modified events. The demand for tickets far exceeds the supply, but track officials have added more seats and 100 acres of additional parking space. What a crowd!

Track Facts

Length: 1.017 miles

Banks: 22° and 25°

Records: Qual: 157.099 mph
Ricky Rudd, 10/94

Race: 130.748 mph
Kyle Petty, 10/92

Schedule: Goodwrench 500, February
Delco 500, October

Tickets: P.O. Box 500, Rockingham, NC
28379, 910-582-2861

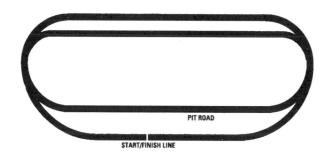

The ROCK traditionally hosts the first and last Winston events in the Carolinas. Also, the world pit crew competition is held there; the title is currently held by the Dupont crew of Jeff Flash Gordon. On its high and wide banks Dale Earnhardt won his 4th race of '94 and clinched his record-tieing 7th Winston Cup Championship. Chris Browning is the GM.

Track Facts

Length: .625 mile

Banks: 14°

Records: Qual: 119.016 mph
Ernie Irvan, 4/94

Race: 107.360 mph
Geoff Bodine, 10/92

Schedule: First Union 400, April
Tyson Holl Farms, October

Tickets: P.O. Box 337, North Wilkesboro,
NC 28659, 910-667-6663

Built in 1947, North Wilkesboro is the oldest charter member in NASCAR. This was the first track ever built with banking and that has led to the style of racing that you experience today. Located in the mountains of North Carolina between the Charlotte and Winston-Salem tracks, it seats 46,000 fans who come here twice a year to see some of the most exciting up-close racing on the Winston Cup Circuit. The track is ably managed by Hank Schoolfield and Mike Staley.

Phoenix International Raceway

Track Facts

Length: 1 mile

Banks: 9-11°

Records: Qual: 129.833 mph
Sterling Marlin, 10/94

Race: 107.463 mph
Terry Labonte, 10/94

Schedule: Slick 50, October

Tickets: P.O. Box 13008, Phoenix, AZ 85002,
602-252-2227

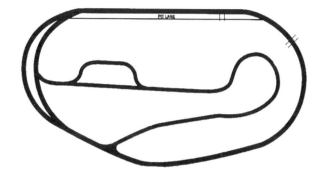

It's the jewel of the Southwest as far as auto racing goes and this track has seen it all. NASCAR, Indy, sports cars, motorcycles, etc. A record crowd of 96,000 saw Terry Labonte and Sterling Marlin set track records. The recently added 11,000 seats were quickly filled and plans are in the works to upgrade again. Buddy Jobe is the man who brings this wide variety of auto racing to the wild West.

Track Facts

Length: 2.5 miles

Banks: 14°, 8°, 6°

Records: Qual: 164.558 mph
Rusty Wallace, 10/94

Race: 144.069 mph
Alan Kulwicki, 7/92

Schedule: UAW-GM 500, June
Miller Genuine Draft 500, July

Tickets: P.O. Box 500, Long Pond, PA 18334
717-646-2300

Pocono Raceway

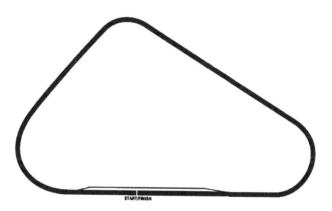

START/FINISH

Slingshot, that no-holds-barred technique that's unique to superspeedway's, is always demonstrated at its best on this tri-oval. Rusty Wallace was doing it constantly in July of '95 till he spun out. Each of the three turns presents it's own special challenges and makes the race very close to a road course. All in all, it never gets boring as even the radio broadcasts seem to pack extra excitement.

Richmond International Raceway

Track Facts

Length: .750 mile

Banks: 14°

Records: Qual: 124.052 mph
Ted Musgrave, 9/94

Race: 107.709 mph
Davey Allison, 3/93

Schedule: UAW-GM 500, June
Miller Genuine Draft 500, July

Tickets: P.O. Box 500, Long Pond, PA 18334
717-646-2300

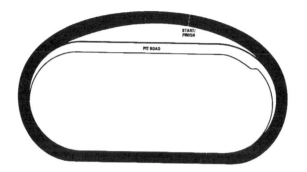

Since 1953 NASCAR has been running hard at Richmond; in 1988 it started running harder as the track was lengthened from its half-mile size to three-fourths of a mile. It's now a large short track and a small Superspeedway. 70,000 fans pour in for the Pontiac Excitement 400 in March to see their favorite throttle jockeys up close at well over 100 mph. The Sawyer family sees to it that everything runs smooth and exciting.

Sears Point Raceway

Track Facts

Length: 2.52 miles

Banks: Road Course

Records: Qual: 91.838 mph
Dale Earnhardt, 5/93

Race: 81.412 mph
Ernie Irvan, 6/92

Schedule: Save Mart 300, May

Tickets: Highways 37 & 121, Sonoma, CA
95476, 800-870-RACE

Sears Point Raceway

A state-of-the-art facility, Sears Point is one of the two road courses on the Winston Tour and the only race they hold in the West. Twelve turns, not all in the same direction, and 2 1/2 miles around, the track keeps both drivers and spectators on their toes. Besides the one Winston event, the track hosts Vintage, IMSA, motorcycle, and drag racing. A recent $3 million upgrade will just add to the excitement.

Talladega Superspeedway

Track Facts

Length: 2.66 miles

Banks: 33°

Records: Qual: 212.809 mph
Bill Elliott, 1987

Race: 186.288 mph
Bill Elliott, 1985

Schedule: Winston Select 500, April
Diehard 500, July

Tickets: P.O. Box 777, Talladega, AL 35160
205-362-9064

Talladega Superspeedway

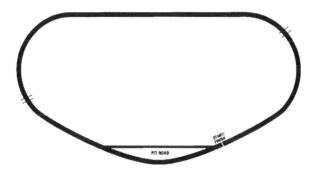

Restrictor plates, those internal engine baffles that are designed to slow 'em down, are a by-product of this place. It is the biggest and fastest track on the circuit. Originally, some drivers balked and said, "No thanks, Bill France. We'll all get killed." The senior Mr. France took a car out to prove it was safe. It seats over 140,000 and is open year-round and is home to the International Motorsports Hall of Fame.

Watkins Glen International

Track Facts

Length: 2.454 miles

Banks: Road Course

Records: Qual: 119.118 mph
Mark Martin, 8/93

Race: 98.752 mph
Mark Martin, 8/94

Schedule: The Bud at the Glen, August

Tickets: P.O. Box 500-T, Watkins Glen, NY
14891, 607-535-2481

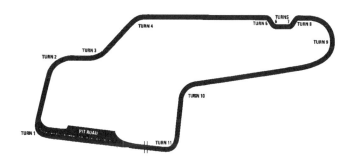

With seven right hand turns in its total of eleven, Watkins Glen offers new challenges to the round-and-round boys, even though NASCAR's been runnin' at the Glen since 1957. I recall my first experience watching Fireball Roberts, Ned Jarrett, Joe Weatherly, and Richard Petty going all over the place in 1964. It's really exciting. Mark Martin has won back-to-back at Watkins Glen and he may do a three-peat this year.

If your local bookstore or souvenir shop is out of **STOCK CAR DRIVERS & TRACKS: Featuring NASCAR's Greatest Drivers!**, and you'd like to have a couple of copies for the guys in the pit, you can order direct by sending a check or money order made payable to PREMIUM PRESS AMERICA for $8.95 ($6.95 plus $2.00 shipping).

Stock Car Books
PREMIUM PRESS AMERICA
P.O. Box 159015
Nashville, TN 37215-9015
(800) 891-7323

Other Premium Press America Stock Car books:

STOCK CAR TRIVIA ENCYCLOPEDIA: The ABC's of Racing!
STOCK CAR FUN & GAMES: Puzzles, Word Games & More!
STOCK CAR LEGENDS: The Laughs, Practical Jokes, and
Fun Stories from Racing's Greats!

For multiple copies and/or more than one title send:

2 books: $11.95 plus $2.00 shipping = $13.95
3 books: $15.95 plus $2.00 shipping = $17.95
4 books: $18.95 plus $2.00 shipping = $20.95

Allow 2-4 weeks for delivery.